Name: _____

PRIMARY
SPELLING
notebook

Primary Paper – space for 20 words per page

ENGLISH PHONOGRAM LIST

a	ai	ar	au	augh
aw	ay	b	bu	c
cei	ch	ci	ck	d
dge	e	ea	ear	ed
ee	ei	eigh	er	es
ew	ey	f	g	gn
gu	h	l	ie	igh
ir	j	k	kn	l
m	n	ng	o	oa
oe	oi	oo	or	ou
ough	ow	oy	p	ph
qu	r	s	sh	si
t	tch	th	ti	u
ui	ur	v	w	wh
wor	wr	x	y	z

Made in the USA
Las Vegas, NV
02 March 2024

86595411R00111